· VOICES ·
from
COLONIAL AMERICA

NORTH CAROLINA

1524 – 1776

MATTHEW C. CANNAVALE

WITH

PATRICK GRIFFIN, PH.D., CONSULTANT

NATIONAL GEOGRAPHIC

WASHINGTON, D.C.

LIBRARY OF CONGRESS CATALOGING-IN-PUBLICATION DATA
Cannavale, Matthew C.
   North Carolina, 1524–1776 / by Matthew C. Cannavale.
      p. cm. — (Voices from colonial America)
   ISBN 978-1-4263-0032-5 (trade)
   ISBN 978-1-4263-0033-2 (library edition)
1. North Carolina—History—Colonial period, ca. 1600–1775—Juvenile literature. I. Title.
   F257.C29 2007
   975.6'02—dc22
                                    2006036004

Printed in Belgium

CONTENTS

North Carolina

COLONY

circa 1755

Extent of North Carolina in 1755
Present-day U.S. state boundary

miles
0   200

INTRODUCTION

by

Patrick Griffin, Ph.D.

A portrait of seven Cherokee chiefs who visited London in 1730 to meet with King George II about trade with Britain. The Cherokee had signed a treaty ceding land to the British in 1721.

Colonial North Carolina's history is America's history. Indeed, stories of settlement, struggle, and development that have defined the ways we understand the experience of the 13 British colonies from their very origins to the Revolution played out in North Carolina. Like Puritan New England and the Chesapeake region, North Carolina's economy, institutions, and culture were shaped by

OPPOSITE: This historical map, created by John Mitchell in 1755, has been colorized for this book to emphasize the boundaries of the North Carolina colony. The inset map shows present-day state boundaries for comparison.

immigrants from the British Isles and their often heroic attempts to adapt Old World ways to the New World.

But another side of America's story is evident in North Carolina as well. Exploitation and conflict went hand-in-hand with settlement and growth. Colonies were planned and planted on the soil of what would be North Carolina by some of the most ruthless visionaries of the early modern Atlantic world—men like Humphrey Gilbert and Walter Ralegh who perfected the art of conquest and settlement in Ireland before attempting them in America. Native American communities that first welcomed European traders in the wake of early adventurers soon had to contend with disease and grew to resent the goods that threatened their survival and traditional way of living.

Founded by favorites of an English king and wealthy planters from the Caribbean, the Carolina colonies became havens for a mix of poor European settlers in search of religious freedom or economic opportunity. Those who settled in the east held the reins of government and enjoyed peace and prosperity while those who settled in the western regions contended with disorder and lack of political power. And, of course, the colony—and later the state—from its beginnings was cursed with the blight of slavery.

Racism and slavery—and the attempts of black men and women to create meaningful lives despite these obstacles—are every bit a part of North Carolina's history as its founding. Indeed, North Carolina's past makes little sense without recognizing that whites struggled for power and status, Indians struggled with the challenges of invasion, and blacks from the Caribbean and from Africa struggled in fields as enslaved laborers.

North Carolina's past, therefore, is full of contradictions. Even the Revolutionary War, which we would expect to be a straightforward fight between Patriots, Loyalists, and British regulars over the issue of independence, deteriorated into a bloody civil war, with brother fighting brother. Yet North Carolina arguably was the place where Americans won their independence. Although the British surrendered farther north at Yorktown, in Virginia, they made their last attempt to win the war in North Carolina. There, British officers failing to recognize the complexities that defined the newly declared state led their troops into a campaign that was destined to fail.

The story of North Carolina's past reminds us that America is a place of contradictions, of promise and despair. Only as we face up to both of these can we come to appreciate who we are. *Voices from Colonial America: North Carolina* will help readers understand this paradox.

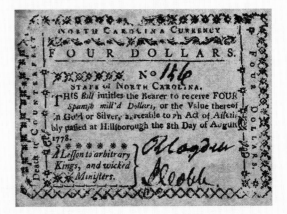

This four-dollar banknote issued by the state of North Carolina in 1778 included the motto A Lesson to arbitrary Kings, and wicked Ministers to remind people that the Revolution was a result of British tax policies that took advantage of the Colonies.

CHAPTER ONE

Early Explorers and Native People

GIOVANNI DA VERRAZANO EXPLORES *the Atlantic coast for France in 1524. Hernando de Soto explores the area in 1539 for Spain.*

y the 1520s, Spanish explorers had claimed Mexico, many of the islands across the Caribbean, and a huge stretch of land that they called Florida—land that included all or parts of what are now the states of Florida, Texas, Georgia, North Carolina, and South Carolina. English and Portuguese explorers,

OPPOSITE: A watercolor by John White, one of the original settlers of Roanoke, illustrates Native Americans spearfishing and traveling in a hollowed-out log canoe in the plentiful waters off North Carolina.

fishermen, and whalers had visited the land and waters off the coast of present-day Newfoundland, Canada. But no one knew for sure that the northern and southern regions were connected.

In the winter of 1523, Giovanni da Verrazano, an Italian privateer, was hired by King Francis I of France to explore the area between Newfoundland and Spanish Florida. His goal was to find an open water passage that would allow him to sail from the Atlantic to the Pacific Ocean and from there to trading destinations in Asia.

privateer—a pirate hired by a government to attack and rob the ships of enemy countries

The king supplied Verrazano with four ships and more than a hundred men. He planned to depart from the French port city of Dieppe and sail south along the coast of Spain to northern Africa before crossing the Atlantic. Shortly after leaving Dieppe, he lost two of his ships in a storm and was forced to travel to Brittany, in France, to repair his remaining ships, the *Delfina* and the *Normanda*. When repairs were completed, he again sailed south. Along the Spanish coast he

Giovanni da Verrazano

attacked several Spanish merchant ships. Finding their cargo valuable, he had it loaded onto the *Normanda*, sent the ship back to Dieppe, and continued his voyage aboard the *Delfina*.

Verrazano's ship departed from the coast of northern Africa on January 17, 1524, with 50 men and enough food and other supplies for an eight-month voyage. After more than 40 days at sea, the crew sighted land at present-day Cape Fear, North Carolina. In his report of the voyage, Verrazano wrote: *"there appeared a new land which had never been seen before by any man, either Ancient or modern. . . . At first it appeared to be rather low-lying; having approached within a quarter of a league, we realized that it was inhabited, for huge fires had been built on the seashore."*

league—a unit of nautical measure, equal to approximately 3 miles (4.8 km)

sandbar—a mound of sand built up by currents in shallow water

barrier island—a long, often narrow island that protects the mainland from strong wave action

Sandbars and barrier islands prevented the ship from approaching the mainland. Verrazano sailed south along the coast in search of a safe harbor for his ship but was not able to find one. After several days, he began to fear that he would run into Spanish forces. So he returned north and dropped anchor several miles out to sea.

He sent men ashore in a small boat to search for natives and to find fresh water. On shore his men encountered Indians. Although Verrazano probably remained aboard the *Delfina*, he described the Native Americans based on the reports of his men:

"They go completely naked except that around their loins they wear skins of small animals. . . . Some of them wear garlands of birds' feathers. They are dark in color, not unlike the Ethiopians, with thick black hair, not very long, tied back behind the head like a small tail. As for the physique of these men, they are well proportioned, of medium height, a little taller than we are. They have broad chests, strong arms, and the legs and other parts of the body are well composed. . . .

We could not learn the details of the life and customs of these people because of the short time we spent on land, due to the fact that there were few men, and the ship was anchored on the high seas."

The *Delfina* soon continued north, still searching for a break in the land and a passage to the Pacific. Verrazano reached the present-day Outer Banks, the islands off the coast of what is now called North Carolina. Verrazano mistook the Outer Banks for the mainland of North America and mistook the body of water beyond them (present-day Pamlico Sound) for the Pacific Ocean.

Verrazano sent men ashore again at a place he called Arcadia, near present-day Kitty Hawk, North Carolina. There his men captured a Native American child to take back to Europe. Verrazano continued to follow the coast north, passing Chesapeake Bay and sailing into the Hudson River. He made several more stops, at times trading with local Indians but all the while hoping to locate a passage to the Pacific.

Continuing north, the *Delfina* reached Newfoundland in June 1524. After resupplying, Verrazano returned to France. His report of the region he had explored described in detail a narrow strip of land that he believed separated the Atlantic and Pacific Oceans.

✖✖✖✖✖✖✖✖✖   P R O F I L E   ✖✖✖✖✖✖✖✖✖

Girolamo da Verrazano

Only one other member of Verrazano's crew is known by name, his brother, Girolamo. Girolamo da Verrazano was a cartographer, or mapmaker. He helped Giovanni chart the coast as the *Delfina* sailed past. In 1529, Girolamo produced one of the first complete maps of North America's Atlantic coast. Because Giovanni incorrectly identified Pamlico Sound as the Pacific Ocean, the map shows North America as two large pieces of land connected by a narrow isthmus (*see arrow*). This body of water was labeled on many maps of the time as the "Sea of Verrazano." This error was not corrected until the early 1600s.

NATIVE PEOPLE

At the time of Verrazano's voyage, the area that would become North Carolina was home to more than 30 different Indian tribes. Although each had its own culture and beliefs, each belonged to one of three major language groups: the Iroquoian, Siouan, or Algonquian. The tribes within a group spoke languages similar enough that they could communicate.

The Algonquian village of Pomeiooc, on the island of Roanoke, painted by Englishman John White around 1586, shows wigwams with platforms for beds inside. A palisade surrounds the village. In the center, Indians gather around a fire.

Verrazano and other early explorers encountered only Algonquian tribes who lived along the coast. While other tribes in the region relied on crops for most of their diet, the Algonquian tribes relied on hunting, fishing, and gathering. This group contained about 7,000 Indians belonging to at least 12 different tribes in far-off places, including the Chippewa, the Delaware, and the Powhatan. The Algonquian language group had the fewest tribes in the area, and many of its tribes had small populations as well.

The Iroquoian tribes included the Tuscarora and the Cherokee and were related to the Iroquois Indians who lived farther north between the Adirondack Mountains and Niagara Falls in present-day New York. Nearly 6,000 Tuscarora lived in what is today northeastern North Carolina.

The Tuscarora lived in longhouses, which were made from a frame of logs covered with strips of bark. Many families lived together in longhouses, some of which were more than 200 feet (61 m) long. The Tuscarora farmed corn, beans, and squash. They also fished and hunted for deer and smaller animals. In Tuscarora society when a man married, he went to live with his wife's family. The women owned all private property and managed the fields and daily life in the village. The men often left for months at a time to hunt, fish, or make war with rival tribes.

matrilineal—tracing ancestry through the mother's side of the family

Like the Tuscarora, the Cherokee had a matrilineal society and a diet made up of mostly beans, corns, and squash. They lived in the southern Appalachian Mountains along the western edge of present-day North Carolina. They were the largest tribe in the area, with nearly 10,000 members spread across at least 40 small villages.

Cherokee villages usually contained between 30 and 60 small structures that housed individual families. The Cherokee lived in circular dwellings made of braided branches, similar to upside-down baskets. The braided frames were covered with mud and grasses.

The largest Siouan tribe was the Catawba. They lived in the piedmont area of North Carolina, between the Atlantic coast and the Appalachian Mountains. The Catawba were fierce warriors, feared by many of the other tribes in the area. The Catawba were known for their battle paint and their tradition of flattening the foreheads of their male babies. Male infants were kept in small wooden cribs with a special attachment that pressed on the baby's forehead. Over time, the attachment was tightened, making the baby's forehead flat and broad. Before battle, warriors painted their faces black with a white circle around one eye.

piedmont—hilly land at the base of mountains

More than 50,000 Indians of various tribes lived across the land that would become North Carolina. The population may have been as high as 100,000, but battles with explorers and exposure to diseases that the Europeans carried would soon greatly reduce the Native American population.

HERNANDO DE SOTO

patent—an official document granting the right to explore or colonize an area

In April 1537, Hernando de Soto was given a patent by the king of Spain to explore and colonize Spanish Florida, which then included much of the southeast section of the present-day United States. De Soto left Spain in 1538 with ten ships, more than 600 men, and 200 horses. He stopped in Hispaniola and Havana, Cuba, to pick up additional men before finally landing somewhere near present-day Tampa Bay, Florida, in May 1539 with nearly a thousand men.

De Soto's expedition traveled by horse north and west in search of silver and gold. They passed through what would become Georgia and South Carolina before entering present-day North Carolina in mid-May 1540. De Soto sent small groups ahead of his main force to scout the area, thus reducing the number of surprise attacks by Indians. Finding enough food for his men and horses was a daily concern that brought him into contact with many groups of Indians. He was able to trade with some of the Indians. When trading did not work, he took what he needed by force, leaving a bloody trail behind him.

Several of de Soto's officers kept detailed notes about the expedition. On May 21, 1540, the Spaniards reached a large Cherokee village called Xuala, near present-day Tryon, North Carolina. One of de Soto's officers, Luys

Hernández de Biedma, wrote: *"The next day, they went to Xuala which is a town on a plain between some rivers; its chief was so well provisioned that he gave to the Christians however much they asked for: slaves, corn, little dogs . . . and however much he had."* The "little dogs" were probably opossums.

From Xuala, de Soto headed west, passing present-day Asheville at a place the Cherokee called Guaxule. The Indians in this area had less food. Hernández wrote, *"They found little corn, and for that reason, although the men were tired and the horses very weak, the governor [de Soto] did not stop over two days."*

De Soto's expedition continued west, through present-day Tennessee and much of the southeastern United States. In 1541, de Soto and his men reached a large river that would come to be known as the Mississippi. Shortly afterward, supplies began to run short. De Soto fell ill and died of a fever in June 1542. The members of his expedition deserted, many finding their way to Spanish settlements in present-day Mexico.

In 1566, Pedro de Coronas, a Spanish explorer who was searching for Chesapeake Bay, landed along the North Carolina coast in what is today Currituck County. He briefly explored the coast but did not come across any Indians. This was probably because the Native American population had been destroyed by disease. Spanish explorers carried smallpox and other diseases that the Indians had never been exposed to. Their bodies had not built up natural defenses so the diseases spread quickly from the Spanish to the Indians. Though the number of Indians to die from these diseases is unknown, the death rate may have been as high as three out of every four Indians.

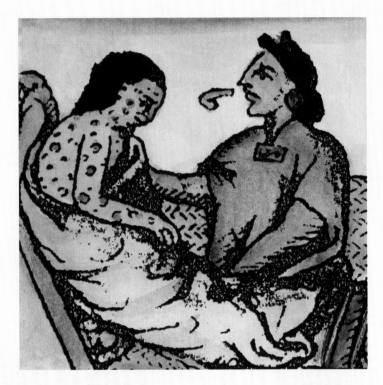

This 16th-century illustration shows an Indian covered with smallpox blisters being treated by the medicine man of the tribe.

By 1570, there were probably fewer than 15,000 Indians living in the land that would become North Carolina. Though both French and Spanish forces had explored the area, neither had been successful in establishing a colony there. The next attempt to colonize the area would come from the English.

CHAPTER TWO

The Colonies at Roanoke

SIR WALTER RALEGH IS GIVEN A PATENT *to colonize what will be part of present-day North Carolina. The Roanoke colony is founded and then "lost."*

I n 1584, Queen Elizabeth gave Sir Walter Ralegh*, an Englishman, accomplished explorer, and writer a patent *"to discover, search, find-out, and view such remote, heathen and barbarous lands, countries, and territories, not actually possessed of any Christian Prince, nor inhabited by Christian People."* The patent gave Ralegh permission to settle and colonize any land he discovered in the name of the Queen and allowed him six years to accomplish this task.

OPPOSITE: Sir Walter Ralegh planned and financed the expedition to Roanoke Island in 1585. Although North Carolina would eventually name its state capital for him, he never set foot in the region.

This spelling reflects the latest scholarly thinking on how Ralegh actually spelled his name.

Ralegh was continuing the work of his half-brother, Sir Humphrey Gilbert, an English military leader and explorer. Gilbert had been granted a patent by Queen Elizabeth in 1578 to explore and colonize North America. He established a colony near present-day Newfoundland, Canada, but during his return to England his ship was lost in a storm.

Sir Humphrey Gilbert, who perished in a storm on a voyage to explore
and establish a colony in the New World for Queen Elizabeth I,
is said to have shouted before his ship was crushed by a giant wave,
"We are as near heaven by sea as by land."

In the spring of 1584, Ralegh hired two captains, Philip Amadas and Arthur Barlowe, and instructed them to find a good location for a colony along the Atlantic coast of North America. On April 27, 1584, they departed from Plymouth, England. They reached North America in early July and sailed along the coast in search of a good harbor. On July 13, they landed nearly 12 miles (19 km) north of present-day Roanoke, North Carolina. They claimed the land in the name of Queen Elizabeth. Then they set out to explore Roanoke Island and the mainland opposite it.

In their report, the captains described the area as *"very sandy and low toward the water"* but abundant in fruits and strong trees for lumber. *"We found such plenty, both on the sand and on the green soil on the hills, as in the plains, as well on every little shrub, as also climbing towards the tops of high Cedars, that I think in all the world the like abundance is not to be found."*

Barlowe and Amadas returned to England with maps they had drawn of the area, samples of the fruits and plants that grew there, and two Indians, named Wanchese and Manteo. According to some records, the Indians chose to accompany Barlowe and Amadas. It is more likely that they were captured and forced to travel to England.

Both Ralegh and Queen Elizabeth were impressed by Amadas and Barlowe's discovery. The Queen named the new land Virginia. Part of this land would later become the colony of North Carolina.

THE FIRST ROANOKE COLONY

Ralegh quickly began making plans for a larger group to sail to the area and establish a colony. He hired his cousin, Sir Richard Grenville, an experienced naval commander, to lead the expedition.

On April 9, 1585, seven ships departed from Plymouth, England, for Roanoke Island. The ships carried 108 settlers, all male, including some members of Amadas and Barlowe's crew and Amadas himself. Also on board were Wanchese and Manteo, who would serve as translators for the Englishmen. The other settlers were workers needed to establish the new colony. John White, an artist, and Thomas Harriot, a scientist, were also part of the expedition.

As the English land at Roanoke, they are greeted by Native Americans along the shoreline.

PROFILE

Thomas Harriot

English scientist Thomas Harriot studied geology, physics, mathematics, astronomy, and linguistics. He experimented on the soil, rocks, and minerals found in the Roanoke area. He reported back to Ralegh that the soil would be profitable for crops and that the rocks and minerals of the area would have some value. He also studied the Algonquian language and learned to speak it. This ability allowed him to learn a great deal about the nearby tribes. Although Harriot respected the natives, he still considered them savages. He wrote to Ralegh, *"It may be hoped, if means of good government be used,"* that the local Indians *"may in short time be brought to civility and the embracing of true religion."*

During the voyage, the expedition attacked and raided two Spanish merchant ships and took some of their cargo and supplies for the English colonists' own use.

On June 26, 1585, the members of the expedition sighted present-day Cape Hatteras. They sailed south and landed on what today is Ocracoke Island. There they set up a temporary camp, then spent the next month exploring neighboring islands and the coast. Grenville selected a location at the north end of Roanoke Island as the site for his colony.

Shortly after the English settlers arrived, a report came to Grenville that an Indian had stolen a silver cup from one of the colonists. His men located the accused Indian, who was a member of the Sectoan tribe, called Roanoke by the English. They followed him back to Aquascogok, an Indian village not far from the English settlement. Rather than trying to resolve the situation peacefully, Grenville ordered his men to burn the village to the ground. Grenville knew that there were far more Indians than English in the area. He believed that the best way to prevent further thefts or attacks by the Indians was to show how fierce the English response would be.

The Sectoan flee their village after Sir Richard Grenville ordered English settlers to burn it to the ground as punishment for the theft of a silver cup.

English military officers like Grenville and Ralegh had reputations among their countrymen for being ruthless soldiers. Their vicious treatment of people England had warred with in Ireland would foretell the cruelty that would befall many Indians who encountered the English in America.

Shortly after this incident, Grenville selected Ralph Lane to serve as governor of the colony, and Grenville returned to England to get additional supplies.

Lane was an experienced adventurer and government official. He set his men to work constructing a wooden fort that he called the New Fort in Virginia. The fort was star-shaped, and the houses of the settlers were built outside its walls. The colonists made bricks from the clay-rich soil and used them to reinforce the fort and to construct their houses—some of which were two stories high.

Lane realized the importance of developing peaceful relationships with the Indians. Writing to a friend in England, Lane described the Indians as *courteous, and very desirous to have clothes.* The colonists traded English clothing and small copper trinkets to the Indians. In exchange, the Indians gave whatever extra food they could spare through the summer and autumn to the colonists and taught them how to make fish traps. As the seasons changed, however, the Indians had fewer crops to share with the colonists. The hungry English grew angry when the Indians refused to share their limited rations.

Some colonists captured Indians and ransomed them back to the tribe for food. In turn, the natives began destroying the fish traps they had helped the colonists set up.

With food running out, Lane divided his men into small groups and sent them to live on other islands or along the mainland. He hoped they would be able to find enough food to survive until Grenville returned with supplies. On June 9, 1586, word reached Lane that Sir Francis Drake, a well-known English privateer, had anchored off the coast of Roanoke with a fleet of 23 ships. Drake offered either to supply the colony with a ship and enough food for two months or to transport all the colonists back to England. Lane asked for the ship and the supplies. When a storm destroyed the ship and the provisions, Drake offered another ship and more supplies. This time, however, Lane chose Drake's offer of passage back to England. The first English colony at Roanoke was abandoned on June 18, 1586.

Several weeks after the colonists left Roanoke with Drake, a supply ship sent by Ralegh arrived at the colony. Finding it abandoned, the ship and its crew returned to England. Grenville finally returned to Roanoke with three ships in August. On discovering the colony abandoned, Grenville wrote that he was *unwilling to loose the possession of the country which Englishmen had so long held.* So he decided to leave a group of 15 volunteers behind with enough supplies to last two years. He then returned to England.

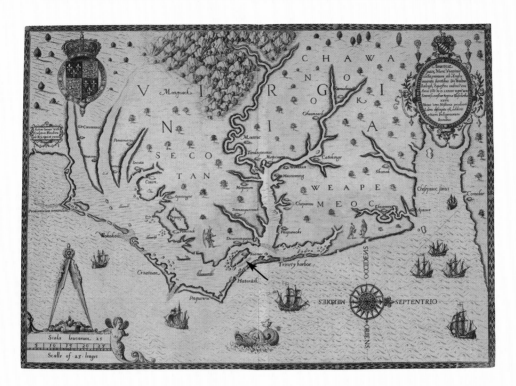

A Map of Virginia, engraved by John White, appears in Thomas Harriot's
book *A briefe and true report of the new found land of Virginia*, 1590.
An arrow marks the location of Roanoke Island.

THE LOST COLONY

In 1587, Ralegh organized a second expedition to Virginia.
He planned to have his settlers establish a colony north of
Roanoke near Chesapeake Bay, where natural harbors protected ships from storms and the open ocean. By offering
each man who made the trip 500 acres (203 ha) of land in
Virginia, he recruited 150 people, including 17 women and
nine children. Ralegh believed this colony would become a
permanent settlement.

Unlike the first colony, which was ruled by a single governor with all land owned by Ralegh or the Queen, the new colony was run by a governor and a committee of 12 assistants. This governing body became known as the Governor and Assistants of the City of Ralegh in Virginia. John White, the artist who had been a member of the original Roanoke expedition, was appointed governor.

On May 8, 1587, three ships under the direction of White departed from Plymouth, England. The ships sailed south to pick up the trade winds off the coast of Africa and then crossed the Atlantic. Sailing past the island of Hispaniola and then north along the Atlantic coast, they arrived at Roanoke on July 22.

White and several colonists headed to the fort, hoping to meet with the 15 men Grenville had left the year before. They soon discovered that the fort had been

VIRGINIA DARE

The First English Child Born in North America

VIRGINIA DARE WAS THE FIRST child born in North America to English parents. She was born on the morning of August 18, 1587, the daughter of Eleanor and Anaias Dare and the granddaughter of Governor White. Though her birth was recorded, few other details are known. Nine days after her birth, Governor White returned to England for supplies. He would never see his daughter, Eleanor, his granddaughter, Virginia, or the other Roanoke colonists again.

destroyed, although the houses remained. Nearby, they found the bones of one man, but no sign of the others. White described the scene: *"the houses stand unhurt, save that the nether [lower] rooms of them, and also of the fort, were overgrown with melons of diverse sorts, and deer within them, feeding on those melons."*

Since it was already late July, White decided to have the colonists settle near the fort. They would use the existing houses and build new ones as needed for protection against the coming winter.

Shortly after work began, George Howe, one of the 12 assistants to the governor, and several other men were captured and killed by Indians. White was able to contact the Indian Manteo, whom he had befriended earlier. Manteo helped the colonists track down the Indians who killed Howe. He identified them as members of the Roanoke tribe who lived in a town called Dasamonquepeuc on southern Roanoke Island.

White prepared to attack the village, but word of the English plan reached the Indians, and they fled. News of their retreat reached the Croatoan, a peaceful tribe living on nearby Croatoan Island. A group of Croatoan traveled to Dasamonquepeuc, hoping to salvage any crops or supplies that the fleeing Roanoke had left behind. White and his force attacked, not realizing they were slaughtering the peaceful Croatoan. Thanks to Manteo, who was able to explain what had happened, the Croatoan resumed their peaceful relationship with the Roanoke settlers.

By mid-August, provisions were running low. Governor White decided to take a small crew and the three ships back to England for supplies. He instructed those who stayed behind that if they left Roanoke, they should carve the name of their destination on a tree, somewhere easily visible. If they were forced to leave because of an attack, they should carve a cross above the name of the location.

On August 27, White left Roanoke with his three ships. Reaching London, he found that England was at war against Spain. All available ships, men, and supplies were needed for the war.

White finally returned to Roanoke three years later on August 16, 1590. Traveling with a party of 25 men, White found the settlement abandoned and the houses dismantled. Trees had been cut into spikes and planted in a circular wall like a fort. The entire area was overgrown with tall grasses. Inside the ring of trees the newcomers found a large tree with the word "CROATOAN" carved into its bark. Since there was no cross carved above it, White assumed that the colonists must have decided to move to Croatoan Island.

The next day he attempted to sail to Croatoan, but a storm blew the ship out to sea. He decided to sail to England rather than risk trying to return to the island in the storm. During the voyage, he wrote that the carving on the tree was a *"certain token"* that his daughter and granddaughter, along with the other colonists, had survived. White became ill and died three years later, never returning to North America.

In 1603, Queen Elizabeth I died. James I was crowned King of England. King James did not like Ralegh. Fearing that he was too powerful, he was accused of being disloyal to the crown. Ralegh was imprisoned in the Tower of London from 1603 until he died in 1616.

Finding the Lost Colony

SEVERAL EXPEDITIONS FROM JAMESTOWN SEARCHED FOR the Roanoke colonists, but they were never found. Even today, no one knows for sure what happened to them. Many historians believe that neighboring Indian tribes killed the colonists or that the Spanish sailed north from Florida and captured them. Other historians think that the English settlers left the colony, moved inland, and eventually were taken in by Indian tribes. Still others suggest that a hurricane or outbreak of disease wiped out the colony.

charter—a written guarantee of rights

In 1606, King James gave a group of investors who called themselves the Virginia Company of London a charter to establish a colony in Virginia. In 1607, they established Jamestown, in honor of the king. It was the first lasting English colony in the New World.

CHAPTER THREE

Trade, Tobacco, and the Carolina Colony

KING CHARLES II GIVES EIGHT MEN *control of land he calls Carolina. Colonists seem reluctant to settle. The proprietors resort to giving land to anyone willing to travel south.*

I n 1492, when Christopher Columbus, an Italian explorer sailing for Spain, first landed in the Caribbean, he traded with the natives for *"fruit, wooden spears, and certain dried leaves which gave off a distinct fragrance."* He had no idea what the "dried leaves" were and discarded them after returning to his ship. Eventually, after

OPPOSITE: Small plots of tobacco were first planted and cultivated by indentured servants and black slaves on plots close to town.

THE FIRST CAROLINA

In 1625, King James I died. He was succeeded by King Charles I, who, in 1629, gave a patent for discovery and colonization of the land south of Virginia to Sir Robert Heath, a friend and adviser. The land was named Carolina to honor King Charles, whose name in Latin is Carolus.

King Charles did not get along with many of the leaders of Parliament. He believed that, as King, he had the right to powers that Parliament wanted to limit. This disagreement divided England and pulled the country into civil war. Parliament eventually won the struggle, and Charles was found guilty of treason and beheaded in 1649. After the King's execution, Sir Robert Heath was stripped of the patent and fled England.

watching the natives, Columbus and other explorers learned to smoke and chew these leaves, which were called tobacco. They took tobacco back to Europe, where a demand soon grew. The Spanish and Portuguese established large tobacco plantations in the Caribbean and in South America and began exporting tobacco to Europe.

Within a year of founding Jamestown, colonists began exporting tobacco. But the Virginia tobacco was *"poor and weak and of a biting taste."* In 1612, John Rolfe began mixing tobacco seeds native to Virginia with seeds from the West Indies. He developed a *"sweet-scented"* blend that soon became more popular than Spanish and Portuguese tobaccos. Demand for tobacco from Virginia soared, and Jamestown prospered. The colonists began importing slaves from Africa to work in the tobacco fields. New colonists also

emigrate—to leave a country and move to another

emigrated from England to Virginia. Settlers began to move into Indian lands along the present-day Virginia–North Carolina border.

In September 1651, Colonel Edward Bland of Virginia led an expedition of 100 English soldiers along with Indian scouts and translators south from Jamestown. He hoped to find more land well-suited to growing tobacco. He explored the area near present-day Albemarle and Pamlico Sounds and described it as *"far more temperate than ours of Virginia"* and *"a land in which Tobacco will grow larger and in more quantity."*

Colonists near the southern border of Virginia began crossing into present-day northeastern North Carolina. Tobacco grown there soon became a profitable export. Unfortunately, there were no established ports in the area so tobacco grown there could not be shipped directly to England. Instead, it had to be shipped through Virginia.

Wagons carry barrels of dried tobacco leaves to be loaded for export on ships along the James River in Virginia.

CHARLES II AND THE CAROLINA COLONY

Back in England, Charles II, son of King Charles I, became King in 1660. He rewarded many of those who helped him regain the throne of England with gifts of land or titles. Eight of his supporters were granted control of the land within the limits prescribed by the charter.

King Charles described the land:

> *All that Territory or tract of ground, situate, lying, and being within our Dominions in America, extending from the North end of the Island called Luck Island, which lies in the Southern Virginia Seas and within six and Thirty degrees of the Northern Latitude, and to the West as far as the South Seas [Pacific Ocean]; and so Southerly as far as the River Saint Mathias, which borders upon the Coast of Florida, and within one and Thirty degrees of Northern Latitude, and West in a direct Line as far as the South Seas aforesaid. . . .*

He gave each man the title Lord Proprietor and called the land Carolina, as his father had years earlier. The grant included all land extending west from the region's Atlantic boundary.

The proprietors divided the land into three counties: Albemarle, Clarendon, and Craven. Albemarle already had some English colonists—the farmers who had moved south from Virginia. The proprietors appointed William

Drummond, a Scottish merchant, governor of Albemarle County. Governors were not appointed for Clarendon or Craven since, at the time, no Europeans lived there.

While some of the proprietors lived in other English colonies, most remained in England. In addition to Drummond, there was an appointed council to help with governing. The proprietors believed that most colonists did not know enough about how to build or govern a colony and that it was best to make important decisions without consulting the settlers.

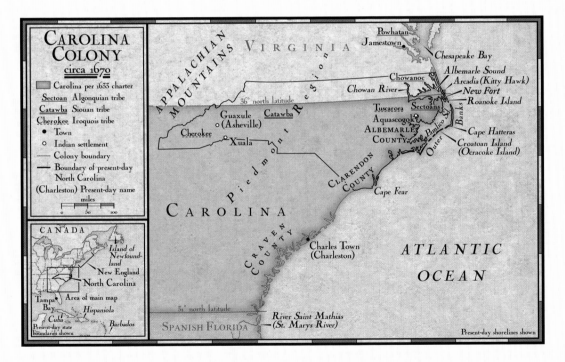

According to its 1663 charter, England's Carolina Colony stretched from Virginia to Spanish Florida. By 1670, there were three main areas of settlement: Albemarle County—across Pamlico Sound from the abandoned Roanoke colonies—Cape Fear, and the area around the port city of Charles Town. Native Americans lived throughout the region, but only the main tribes that lived in what is now North Carolina (dark outline) are shown.

SETTLEMENTS *on* Cape Fear

BEGINNING IN 1663, SEVERAL groups of colonists from New England and the island of Barbados (an English territory in the Caribbean) attempted to settle near Cape Fear, in southeastern Clarendon County. None of these settlements lasted long. Most failed because supplies ran out or because hurricanes destroyed crops and buildings. On August 27, 1667, a particularly strong hurricane swept across the area, destroying nearly all the remaining settlements. Most of the surviving settlers moved back north, settling in Albemarle or returning to New England.

Many of the people in Albemarle County, who had lived in Carolina before the proprietors took control of the area, believed that they could govern themselves. In 1665, the colonists elected their first assembly. Although the assembly was officially a part of the governing system, the proprietors and their appointed officials did not have to follow its suggestions.

By the middle 1660s, Albemarle County contained little more than scattered tobacco farms and small lumbering and trading operations. The people of Albemarle knew that in order for the colony to succeed they needed to attract more settlers. On May 1, 1668, in what became known as the "Great Deed Grant," the proprietors decided to give Carolina settlers the same type of land grant that was given in Virginia. Since 1619, Virginia colonists who paid their own way to

Virginia had been granted 50 acres (20 ha) of land. Each member of a family, including women and children, could receive this amount of land. For example, a family of four got 200 acres (80 ha), but only an adult male could hold title to the land.

Carolina's proprietors hoped that the offer of land would attract recent settlers from Virginia, as well as colonists from Europe. The land grants encouraged some immigration but not enough. The following year, the proprietors issued a new law stating that colonists who settled in Carolina would not have to pay any colonial taxes for one year and would be forgiven any debts they owed.

title—the right of ownership or possession of property

immigration—moving to a new area where a person is not native

A photograph of a 1757 land grant given to Gilbert Strahorn in Prestwoods Creek. The small map at the top of the document shows the boundaries of his 570 acres (230 ha), which begin at a poplar tree.

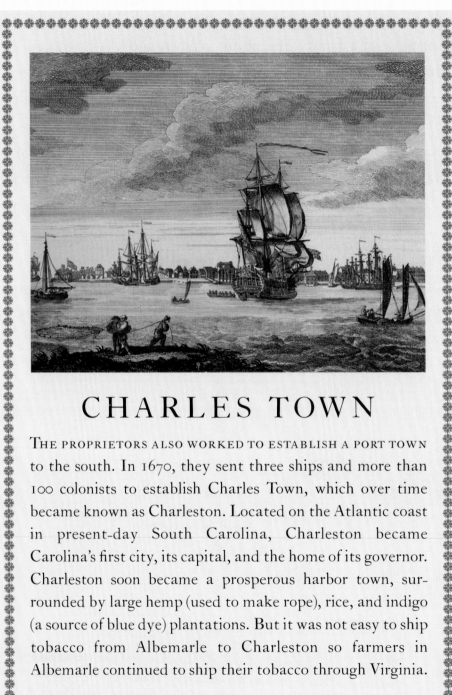

CHARLES TOWN

THE PROPRIETORS ALSO WORKED TO ESTABLISH A PORT TOWN to the south. In 1670, they sent three ships and more than 100 colonists to establish Charles Town, which over time became known as Charleston. Located on the Atlantic coast in present-day South Carolina, Charleston became Carolina's first city, its capital, and the home of its governor. Charleston soon became a prosperous harbor town, surrounded by large hemp (used to make rope), rice, and indigo (a source of blue dye) plantations. But it was not easy to ship tobacco from Albemarle to Charleston so farmers in Albemarle continued to ship their tobacco through Virginia.

While this law did attract some honest, hardworking colonists who struggled to pay their debts, it also attracted many thieves and dishonest people who had built up large debts in Virginia and wanted to avoid paying them. In Virginia, Albemarle County soon became known as "Rogue's Harbor."

Colonists continued to move into Albemarle County, but few towns were formed. Instead, the area slowly filled with small farms and plantations. The population became divided between colonists who supported the proprietors and those who supported the assembly. New settlers tended to support the proprietors because of the land grants they offered, while colonists who had lived in Carolina longer tended to support the assembly.

indentured servants—
people who agreed to work for a certain period of time in exchange for paid passage to a colony

People who had the money to operate large farms often employed indentured servants or slaves. At first, most black slaves in the Carolinas were brought from the Caribbean. They were outnumbered by white indentured servants until the middle 1700s, when farms and plantations grew and slave traders began bringing slaves from Africa to work Carolina's tobacco fields. By 1775, blacks, who were primarily slaves, made up the largest ethnic group in the Colonies. By 1790, one out of four people living in North Carolina owned slaves. Harsh laws called slave codes, passed in 1696, governed the brutal way slaves could and would be treated in the years to come.

SLAVERY

As living conditions for poorer people in Europe improved in the mid-1700s, fewer were willing to travel to America as indentured servants. At the same time, slave trade from Africa increased. Soon slaves became the preferred form of labor on Carolina's farms and plantations.

Slaves were property and as such had no legal rights. Owners could do almost anything they wanted to a slave. While some owners provided adequate housing and food for their slaves, most did not. Slaves were frequently punished and beaten. Families were torn apart when husbands, wives, and children were sold to new owners and sent away to live and work on another plantation. Slaves were not allowed to learn to read or write, and they were barred from assembling in groups in order to discourage uprisings. The average slave cost 40 pounds (the monetary unit of Great Britain) to purchase, but earned his or her owner more than 40 pounds in less than a year. They worked from sunrise to sunset, with little food and water in between.

Slavery grew most quickly in and around Charleston. Rice plantations in the region required a lot of labor to grow and harvest. It was backbreaking work, and without slaves it was difficult to make money. Conditions in the wet rice fields were grim and many slaves contracted deadly diseases carried by mosquitoes. It was cheaper for owners to work their slaves to death and then replace them, than to take care of them.

Slavery spread quickly up the coast from Charleston. In addition to rice plantations, slavery helped indigo and tobacco plantations grow and prosper.

ENGLAND IMPOSES TAXES

In 1673, the English government passed the Plantation Duty Act. This law required Carolina and the other English colonies to trade directly with England. If colonists traded directly with other colonies, they faced fines and heavy taxes. This law angered many people in Albemarle. The area did not have a deep harbor for trading ships so it was impossible for people there to trade directly with England. Instead, they had to ship their tobacco to another colony, usually Virginia. From Virginia it could be sent to England. This meant that the Carolina colonists had to pay additional taxes and fees.

Acting governor John Jenkins refused to fine farmers and merchants for not shipping their tobacco directly to England. His leniency pleased some colonists but angered others, further dividing the people of Carolina. In 1675, Thomas Eastchurch and Thomas Miller, both respected public leaders, spoke out against Governor Jenkins. In response, he had them arrested for treason and imprisoned.

The assembly reviewed the charge of treason. After a month of debate, it decided that Jenkins was the one who had committed treason and had him imprisoned. Eastchurch and Miller were freed. By March 1676, however, the assembly, deciding that Jenkins had acted justly, released him from prison and made him governor again. His term would not last long.

Despite these problems, Carolina remained profitable, exporting 2,000 hogsheads of tobacco in 1677. Those 2,000 hogsheads would make a square pile of tobacco more than 1 mile (1.6 km) high and a mile long on each side.

hogshead—a large barrel with a 63 gallon (238 l) capacity

Meanwhile, Eastchurch and Miller traveled to London and convinced the proprietors that they should run the colony. As acting governor, Miller tried to force people to obey the law by increasing the taxes on tobacco. This move angered most of the colonists.

Thomas Miller stands in a black hat, hands bound, surrounded by armed colonists following the orders of John Culpeper and George Durant to arrest him.

In December 1679, John Culpeper and George Durant, two well-known political leaders in Carolina, captured Miller, and imprisoned him. Culpeper became the official tax collector, though he did not actually collect the tax on tobacco. Durant and other supporters joined the assembly and ran the colony successfully without a governor for 18 months.

In the summer of 1680, Culpeper was arrested in England while trying to negotiate with the proprietors. The court records note that he was one *"of the Principall Contrivers & Promoters of rebellion." Culpeper was tried, found "guilty of Treason in abetting and encouraging a Rebellion in Carolina,"* and sentenced to prison. Culpeper was eventually released and returned to Albemarle, but he he avoided politics thereafter.

The ten years that followed saw the colony overseen by three different governors. In 1689, the proprietors appointed Philip Ludwell governor of Carolina. Like other governors, he lived in Charleston. Realizing that life in Charleston was quite different from life in Albemarle, he appointed John Gibbs as deputy governor of Carolina. Gibbs oversaw the northern portion of the colony, from Cape Fear to the north and west, including Albemarle County. People soon began calling the two regions North and South Carolina, but it would be more than 20 years before the Carolina colony would officially split. ✳

CHAPTER FOUR

Encounters With Indians and Pirates

INDIANS STRUGGLE TO MAINTAIN THEIR LAND
*but are soon overpowered by the colonists. The towns
of Bath and New Bern prosper.*

As the number of English and other European settlers increased in Albemarle County, many Indians native to the area retreated from their homelands and moved south. Others were captured and sold as slaves. The Chowanoc engaged in an unsuccessful year-long battle with English settlers in 1675, and were eventually confined to a 12-square-mile (31-sq-km) plot of

OPPOSITE: This engraving shows a Tuscarora warrior wearing a fox pelt draped across his body, ready for battle.

land near the Chowan River. The years that followed would see uprisings with other tribes. The results were always disastrous for the Indians. By 1700, fewer than 500 Native Americans remained in Albemarle County. At the same time, African slaves continued to escape from plantations in Virginia and flee to the south into North Carolina and beyond.

In August 1700, John Lawson, an English surveyor and amateur botanist, traveled from London to Charleston, still the only town in the Carolina colony. He had taken a position as official surveyor of the colony and hoped to survey areas in

surveyor—a person who examines land and determines its borders

botanist—a person who studies plants

Carolina for new settlement. Upon arriving, he admired Charleston's *"very regular and fair streets"* lined with *"good buildings of brick and wood."* But he soon realized that English settlement in the area did not extend inland much farther than 40 miles (64 km) from the Atlantic coast.

Hiring six Englishmen and four Indians to serve as translators and guides, Lawson left Charleston on December 28, 1700, heading inland and then north. Over the next 60 days, he and his party crossed Carolina, traveling more than 550 miles (885 km), as far as the north bank of the Pamlico River. Four years later he returned to the area. Finding it sparsely settled, he purchased 60 acres (24 ha) on which he established Bath, the first town in what would become North Carolina.

Lawson studied animals, insects, and many types of plants. He also observed the local Indians in great detail, hoping to learn about their way of life. Years later, he wrote about his adventures and discoveries in a book titled *The History of Carolina*, which became popular in England. Of the Indians, Lawson wrote: *"They are really better to us than we are to them; they . . . take care we are armed against hunger and thirst: we do not do so by them . . . but let them walk by our doors hungry."*

An illustration from John Lawson's book shows a variety of wildlife in North Carolina, including buffalo, snakes, terrapins (a type of turtle), opossums, bobcats, deer, bears, and raccoons.

Lawson also noted the decline in the Indian populations of the area, writing: *"[Local Indians were] formerly a large nation, though now, very much decreased since the English hath seated their Land . . . Wherever the Europeans go, the Indians are apt to catch distemper [illness or disease] the Europeans carry. The smallpox has destroyed many thousands of these natives, who no sooner than they are attacked with the violent fevers . . . fling themselves overhead into the water."*

Bath grew and prospered. By 1707, the town's port had become an important shipping location for tobacco and naval stores. By 1708, there were 12 houses and at least 50 colonists. News of the success of Bath spread. Baron Christoph von Graffenried, a Swiss investor, was impressed by the success of Bath. He traveled to London to meet John Lawson, who was there overseeing the publication of his book. Graffenreid received permission from the proprietors to establish a town in Carolina, and Lawson agreed to help him find a good location.

Graffenried gathered a group of Swiss and German colonists and traveled to Bath. From Bath they headed south as Lawson instructed and settled at the meeting of the Trent and Neuse Rivers. Graffenried called the town New Bern, after his home of Bern, Switzerland. The area was already the location of a small Tuscarora town called Chattoka. Graffenried paid the Chattoka

THE NAVAL STORES ACT

In 1705, the English Parliament passed the Naval Stores Act. England had long depended on importing from other nations the tar, hemp, and other goods—called naval stores—needed to build ships. These goods could be grown, harvested, or produced in many of the Colonies, but they were not as profitable export items as tobacco or lumber. Under the Naval Stores Act, England agreed to pay an additional fee for each shipment of naval stores from the Colonies. Farmers soon found that hemp grew well in the coastal areas of Carolina. They also found that bark from many trees in the region could be heated to release tar. Many merchants and entrepreneurs soon set up tar and hemp companies.

Indians for the land. Although the natives moved into the wilderness, many members of the tribe were dissatisfied with the payment and arrangement. New Bern soon grew into a prosperous port town surrounded by hemp and tobacco fields.

The new colonists traded with the Indians, but were often unfair. One merchant in New Bern noted that the colonists *"cheated these Indians in trading, and would not allow them to hunt near their plantations."*

In early September 1711, Lawson invited Graffenried to join him on an expedition. Traveling too close to Indian hunting grounds, the men were captured and taken to Catechna, the town of the Tuscarora leader King Hancock. Graffenried was freed, but Lawson, who quarreled with the king, was not as lucky. It is believed that the Tuscarora *"stuck him full of fine small splinters . . . like hogs' bristles, and so set him gradually on fire."*

John Lawson and Baron von Graffenried make a stop along their journey up the Neuse River in search of a quicker route to Virginia. Tuscarora, hiding in the trees, await a strategic moment to capture the two Europeans.

THE TUSCARORA WAR

Before daybreak on September 22, 1711, more than 500 Tuscarora and their Indian allies gathered at Catechna. King Hancock had decided to declare war on the North Carolina colonists. He hoped to retake tribal lands and push the settlers out of the region. Hancock divided the warriors into small groups, and at sunrise they attacked the plantations and towns along the Neuse River. Less than two hours later, more than 130 colonists were dead. Some, mostly women and children, were taken as captives. In the days that followed, the attacks spread to Bath and its surrounding plantations.

allies—countries or groups of people who have agreed to aid and support each other

There were no armed forts in North Carolina, although both New Bern and Bath had some small fortifications to protect colonists who were able to flee there. Colonists watched helplessly as Indians burned their homes, destroyed their fields, and slaughtered their livestock.

fortifications—constructions that help strengthen or defend a location

Edward Hyde, deputy governor of Carolina, wrote to the governor of Virginia and the governor of South Carolina for help. Virginia agreed to stop trading with the Tuscarora and their allies and to send supplies, but it was unable to send troops. Fortunately, South Carolina—by now populated by wealthy planters and merchants—was able to send soldiers and their Indian allies.

In January 1712, Colonel John Barnwell of South Carolina marched north from Charleston with a force of 30 soldiers and more than 500 Indians. Many of the soldiers were volunteers, while many of the Indians were from the Yamassee tribe. He was able to persuade the Yamassee to march with him by agreeing to purchase Tuscarora scalps and captives from the Yamassee. He promised them that they could keep any goods or food they found in Tuscarora villages and arranged to trade British goods and weapons with the Yamassee.

Barnwell reached the Neuse River near a Tuscarora town called Narhantes. Having fought only small groups of Tuscarora, Barnwell saw Narhantes as a good test for his force. His men stormed the town, killing 52 Tuscarora. He was surprised to find that many of the defenders of the village were women, who fought *until most of them are put to the sword.* Barnwell's forces burned the town to the ground and then continued north, reaching Bath on February 10.

In Bath, he was joined by 67 volunteers from other areas in North Carolina. On March 5, they marched on King Hancock's fort at Catechna. After almost two months of battle, King Hancock agreed to a truce.

Over the next year, the truce fell apart, and war again broke out in the area. As before, North Carolina asked South Carolina for aid. In March 1713, a force of nearly 1,000 Yamassee and 33 white soldiers, led by Captain James Moore, marched north from Charleston.

Meanwhile, the Tuscarora and their allies assembled at Fort Neoheroka, an Indian fort in Carolina. By the time Moore and his force reached Neoheroka, more than 1,000 Indians had taken refuge behind its thick walls. On March 20, Moore began three days of constant attack. By the end of the third day, Moore's force had killed more than 500 Tuscarora and taken at least 400 prisoners. The surviving Tuscarora surrendered, ending the Tuscarora War. After the war, most of these Indians traveled north and joined other Iroquois-speaking groups in present-day New York.

Tuscarora warriors travel at night by the light of a torch. North Carolina colonists can be seen hiding in the brush, hoping to avoid the Indians as they pass by.

PIRATES OF
THE OUTER BANKS

Settlers in North Carolina were also in conflict with pirates. What started as privateering often turned into piracy. While privateers were sea captains employed by a country to attack the merchant ships of another country, pirates attacked the merchant ships of any country and took whatever cargo they desired. Many captains who started out as privateers eventually began attacking ships regardless of their country of origin. Pirates did not target only gold and treasure. In fact, most of the cargo that pirates captured was trade goods. Pirates would often capture shipments of food or cloth, then sail into local ports and sell the cargo to the townspeople at very cheap prices. Although the townspeople enjoyed getting such bargains, merchants and government leaders were angered by the pirates' attacks. After the Tuscarora War, when the Indian threat was under control, the British were able to focus on stopping pirates.

Edward Teach was born in Bristol, England, some time before 1700. He gained more fame than any other pirate by attacking ships in the Caribbean and off the Carolina coast. Teach stood more than 6 feet (1.8 m) tall and had a long dark beard, thanks to which he soon became known as Blackbeard. Though no one knows for sure, many historians believe that Blackbeard attacked more than 100 ships.

There is no record of Blackbeard ever killing a person who was not a threat to his life. As long as people aboard the ships that he attacked cooperated, he let them live.

In November 1718, Lieutenant Robert Maynard of the British Navy sailed south from Virginia with two ships. He planned to intercept Blackbeard at his hideout near Ocracoke Island. Blackbeard's ship was anchored between Ocracoke and the mainland. The pirates watched as Maynard's ships, armed with cannons, approached. Just before Maynard came within shooting range, Blackbeard had his men cut the anchor of his ship and steered between sandbars toward the coast. When Maynard followed, both his ships became stuck on sandbars in the shallow water.

After bombarding Maynard's ships, Blackbeard's crew approached one of the marooned ships. Seeing few men on deck, they boarded the vessel. No sooner had Blackbeard and his men reached the deck than Maynard and his crew sprang from hiding places below. Maynard offered Blackbeard and his outnumbered force the chance to surrender, but the pirate refused.

Hand-to-hand fighting broke out on the deck. Men fought with fists, swords, and guns. Maynard shot Blackbeard in the shoulder. Slowed by the wound, the pirate tried to fight his way across the deck toward Maynard. But before he reached Maynard, one of the British crew members slashed Blackbeard's throat. The sailor swung his sword a second time and cut Blackbeard's

head off. When Maynard held up Blackbeard's severed
head, his crew surrendered. Some of the pirates were
released. Others were taken prisoner and hanged. Maynard
kept Blackbeard's head and hung it from the mast of his ship
as a warning to other pirates.

Though other pirates continued to attack ships along
North America's Atlantic coast, no other became as feared
or as famous as Blackbeard. ✻

Edward Teach, also known as Blackbeard, fights in the battle that will
cost him his life in this 19th-century painting by Jean Leon Jerome Ferris.

CHAPTER FIVE

A Royal Colony

NORTH CAROLINA BECOMES A ROYAL COLONY.
*Immigrants from Europe and the northern colonies flock
there for the rich farmland.*

In 1719, the colonists of South Carolina revolted against the proprietors. To end the revolt, King George II of England purchased the South Carolina portion of Carolina from the proprietors and made it a royal colony. In 1729, the King offered to purchase North Carolina as well. All the proprietors except a man named Earl Granville agreed to the sale. Granville retained rights to one-eighth of the colony.

OPPOSITE: A farmer plows a field on a large farm in Salem, North Carolina. The town of Salem, settled in the mid-1700s by Protestants known as Moravians, quickly grew and prospered.

By January 1730, the Royal Colony of North Carolina had a population of more than 35,000. With sales of tobacco, naval stores, and lumber booming, the colony prospered, attracting even more colonists who in turn produced even more goods for export. Immigrants from across Great Britain and other European countries, as well as from the other American colonies headed south from northern ports toward the western regions of North Carolina where land was plentiful. Traveling along the Great Wagon Road, settlers passed through southern Pennsylvania, the present-day Shenandoah Valley, into the piedmont region of western North Carolina. These immigrants, mostly young and poor, formed small communities where they could speak their native languages and maintain the culture of their homelands. Some were the sons and daughters of earlier immigrants who had settled in Pennsylvania and Virginia. All were looking for a chance to prosper in the North Carolina colony.

IMMIGRANTS FROM EUROPE AND THE COLONIES

Hugh Meredith was a Welsh printer, working in Philadelphia, Pennsylvania. When news reached him of land available in North Carolina, he thought about his current job as a printer and wrote, *"I see this as a business I am not fitted for. I was bred a farmer. . . . Many of our Welsh people are going* to settle in North Carolina, where land is cheap. I am inclined to go with them and follow my own employment."

He traveled to a settlement called New Town (present-day Wilmington) near the mouth of the Cape Fear River. Many colonists had recently arrived there from Pennsylvania. He described New Town as *"consisting of not above 10 or 12 scattering mean Houses, hardly worth the name of a village,"* but noted that the town had an excellent harbor that could become a major port. He then described the area's dense pine forests, good pastures, and fertile soil. He sent his descriptions of the area back to the printing shop in Philadelphia, where his former co-workers decided to print them. This encouraged more Welsh to emigrate to Cape Fear in 1731.

Germans who had previously settled in Pennsylvania followed the Welsh in the mid-1740s. Other Germans also emigrated from England. John Martin Bolzius was a German minister who originally settled in Georgia in the 1730s. He wrote to other Germans in Europe to convince them to settle in Georgia and the Carolinas: Many Germans *"arrived very poor, having none but European experience, no honest friends in the land, and because of . . . their errors, no good soil, nor horses or plow. . . . Now, if a man brings some money along into this country and understands economy, or accepts good advice from others who are experienced, he may soon establish himself sufficiently well to lead a pleasant life with his family."* Many settled farther inland from Cape Fear, in the western regions of the colony.

The Moravians emigrated from Pennsylvania and purchased 100,000 acres (40,500 ha) in present-day Forsyth County from Earl Granville. They named the land Wachovia, which in German means "peaceful valley." They soon established several small towns.

Moravians—German-speaking Protestant Christians

NEW BERN FLOURISHES

IN 1745, THE NORTH CAROLINA ASSEMBLY SELECTED NEW BERN as the capital. This choice was made without the delegates from Albemarle in attendance because a storm had kept them from making the trip to New Bern. Because of this, many people in Albemarle refused to pay taxes for years to come.

In 1749, New Bern became the home of the colony's first printing press when James Davis opened a print shop. He busied himself printing government documents and in 1751 began publishing the *North Carolina Gazette*, the first newspaper in the colony.

In 1765, the New Bern Academy opened. The colonial government paid part of the costs of running the school. In exchange, the school agreed to educate ten poor children without charge. This arrangement made the academy the oldest public school in North Carolina.

In 1734, Gabriel Johnston became governor of North Carolina. A native of Scotland, he believed that the Cape Fear area would make a good home for countrymen who wanted to find a fresh start in the New World. Pamphets were spread throughout Scotland.

One pamphlet read: North Carolina can *"produce the same things as . . . Virginia, and in greater perfection . . . . Vegetation is amazingly quick in the province; the soil, in general will produce most things . . . [and] the land . . . is easily cleared . . . Young healthy Negroes can be bought there for between 25 and 40 pounds. Five of these will clear and labour a plantation the first year, so as you shall have everything in abundance for your family, with little trouble to yourself."* In late 1739, a single ship, the *Thistle*, delivered more than 350 Scottish immigrants to New Town. By 1775, at least 25,000 Scots were living in and around Cape Fear.

Settlers from Ireland also emigrated to Pennsylvania and then made their way into North Carolina. Primarily from Ulster in northern Ireland, the majority were Protestant and many settled in the Cape Fear region, creating communities of Scots and Irish.

Most of these immigrants became farmers. Land was plentiful, and they had worked on farms in their native countries. Although few held positions of power in North Carolina, they would grow to be a major influence on the politics of the region.

RELATIONS WITH THE CHEROKEE

Since 1721, North Carolina colonists had been at peace with the Cherokee and most of the other Iroquois-speaking tribes in North Carolina. They agreed on boundaries between each other's settlements and had become close trading partners. In 1754, the Cherokee agreed to allow the British to build outposts on their land and pledged their support in defense of the colonists. Tribes that were enemies of the Cherokee became enemies of the British and, over time, allies of the French.

As immigrants continued to enter North Carolina, colonists began to move into Cherokee land. This upset the Cherokee, but they had grown to depend on British goods, including guns and ammunition. They knew that if they attacked the colonists, trading would stop. Instead of fighting for their land, the Cherokee began moving south into present-day northern Georgia and west into

This Cherokee was one of three chiefs who traveled to England in 1760 to meet with King George III to discuss trade and border issues.

what would become Tennessee. They attacked and overran smaller non-Iroquois tribes that lived in these areas.

In 1755, Edmond Atkin, a merchant who had spent many years trading with various Indian groups across the Carolinas, wrote to the British Government: *"The importance of Indians is now generally known and understood, a Doubt remains not, that the prosperity of our Colonies on the Continent, will stand or fall with our Interest and favor among them. While they are our Friends, they are our Cheapest and strongest Barrier for the protection of our Settlements; when Enemies, they are capable of ravaging in their method of War, in spite of all we can do."* Atkin's understanding of the Indians impressed the British, so they appointed him Superintendent of Indian relations in the South. He worked to control the Indians through trade agreements and treaties.

Meanwhile, to the north and the west, the British and their Iroquois allies were on the brink of war with the French and their Indian allies. Both Great Britain and France claimed the land, then known as the Ohio Territory, west of the Appalachians. The French had explored the Mississippi River and claimed the area around it. The British also claimed the land based on agreements with the Iroquois, who were the largest Indian group in the area.

In October 1753, Major George Washington of Virginia, who would later become the first President of the United States, was sent to meet Jacques Legardeur de Saint-Pierre, the French leader in the Ohio Territory. Saint-Pierre politely received Washington and his troops at a French fort at the western edge of present-day Pennsylvania. Washington read from a letter that the royal governor of Virginia had prepared for him: *"By whose authority [have the French] invaded the King of Great Britain's territories? It becomes my duty to require your peaceable departure."* Saint-Pierre replied, *"As to the summons you send me to retire, I do not think myself obliged to obey."*

In May 1756, Britain declared war on France. Though most of the fighting in North America occurred far north and west of North Carolina, the colony sent Cherokee warriors and soldiers to help the British.

Victory seemed assured for the British until, in 1758, the Cherokee ended their alliance. Soldiers from North Carolina and other colonies had often mistreated the Cherokee. The final blow for the Cherokee came when a force that included soldiers from Virginia and North Carolina lost their food and weapons when their rafts sank while crossing a river. The colonists refused to share their supplies. The Cherokee threatened to leave the colonial force and return to their homes. But the colonists turned on the Cherokee, attacking and killing more than 20 of them. The others escaped and spread the news of the colonists' actions. In North Carolina, the Cherokee began a series of attacks in the piedmont region. The colonists took shelter in the Moravian town of Bethabara, where a large fort had been built but received little support from British troops. Cherokee attacks in the region continued.

By 1760, new military leadership had turned the tide of war in favor of the British. They defeated the French, and fighting ended between these two powers in North America. The British now were able to turn their attention to the Cherokee. In early 1761, Colonel James Grant was put in command of 1,200 British soldiers in western North Carolina and South Carolina.

Grant hired Catawba scouts. Soon his army of nearly 3,000 captured 15 Cherokee towns, destroying the food that the Indians needed for the coming winter. Faced with starvation, the Cherokee signed a treaty ending the violence in December 1761. As part of the treaty, the Cherokee turned much of their land in western North and South Carolina over to Britain. In February 1763, France and England signed the Treaty of Paris, officially ending what is known as the French and Indian War. King George III issued a proclamation that set the western boundary of British settlement in order to separate lands belonging to Native Americans and the colonists.

Though Britain had just won the French and Indian War, it still needed to protect the western frontier of its American colonies. Parliament decided to raise an army of 10,000 troops and station them along the Appalachian Mountains to keep peace on the border between the British and the Indian lands. But keeping such an army would be very expensive. Britain's solution would ultimately lead to war and cost the empire its American colonies. ❧

CHAPTER SIX

Tryon and the Regulators

NORTH CAROLINA'S DIVERSE POPULATION *leads to a separation between those living along the frontier in the west and the merchants and plantation owners in the east. Protestors called the Regulators object to taxes imposed by Britain.*

In an effort to raise funds that had been used up by fighting the French and Indian War, Parliament passed the Stamp Act on March 22, 1765. Britain felt justified in taxing the Colonies since the war had been fought, in part, for their benefit. The Stamp Act required colonists to pay a tax on legal documents, newspapers, playing cards, and other printed paper. While the cost of the stamp was small, most colonial assemblies spoke

OPPOSITE: Governor William Tryon leads British troops (in red) and colonial militia (in blue) in a brief battle with the Regulators, colonists who protested taxes in North Carolina.

The Townshend Acts

IN JUNE 1767, CHARLES Townshend, the royal treasurer and an adviser to King George, announced a tax on lead, glass, paint, paper, and tea imported from Britain by the Colonies. This new tax angered many colonists. Many colonial merchants decided to not to buy British goods until the tax was lifted. The colonists reduced their use of the products as much as possible or relied on goods smuggled from other countries.

In March 1770, most of the taxes were repealed, but Britain continued to enforce the tax on tea.

out against the tax. But because the decision to tax came from Parliament, where the colonists had no representation, they had no legal power to fight the unpopular legislation.

The colonists had no choice but to pay the tax. By November, North Carolina and many other colonies ran out of stamped paper. Without the stamped paper, even people willing to pay the tax could not do so. Without stamped paper, ships could not enter or leave port. Deeds and legal documents could not be filed. Newspapers could not be printed. The newly appointed governor of North Carolina, William Tryon, reported to Britain, "all Civil Government is now at a stand [stop]."

In February 1766, a group of North Carolina colonists calling themselves the Sons of Liberty offered to protect captains and merchants who violated the Stamp Act and shipped goods without the proper stamped papers. Soon the port at Brunswick was reopened. Other American colonies followed suit. By the end of March, British officials realized they were unable to enforce the Stamp Act, and it was repealed by Parliament.

TRYON "PALACE"

Between 1735 and 1764, the towns of New Bern, Wilmington, and Bath all took turns as the capital of North Carolina. Governor Tryon believed it was important for the colony to have a permanent capital and residence for the governor. On December 1, 1766, the assembly approved spending 5,000 pounds for a building to be used as the governor's residence and office and as a meeting place for the assembly in the newly proclaimed capital of New Bern.

Tryon ordered an extravagant, ornate house built. Many of the colonists, upset by what they saw as Tryon's waste of money, began to call the mansion Tryon Palace. For other colonists, however, the palace became an object of pride. Many colonists believed it was *the most beautiful building in the Colonies*" and "*a lasting monument to the . . . country.*"

By the time construction was completed in 1770, the governor's mansion cost 15,000 pounds, three times more than it was supposed to cost.

Meanwhile, to the west along the frontier in Orange County, a group of farmers were organizing to protest against unfair taxes. The dishonest tax collectors often charged additional fees that were not officially required. The farmers were angered further when taxes were raised to cover the construction of Tryon Palace.

These settlers in the western or backcountry region of the colony, primarily Germans, Welsh, and Irish, lived a lifestyle quite different from the merchants, political leaders, and plantation owners to the east. Often ridiculed by prejudiced officials, these people had real grievances. Western settlers did not enjoy the same political rights as easterners because corrupt officials made sure they were underrepresented in the Assembly. They had few outlets for trade, and so struggled to support themselves and their families. They lived in fear of Indian attacks, and eastern officials did little to protect them.

Charles Woodmason, a merchant from Charleston, South Carolina, traveled through the area and noted: "*They are the lowest pack of wretches my eyes ever saw. . . as wild as the very deer. . . . How would the polite people of London stare, to see the females . . . barefoot and bare legged—without caps or handkerchiefs . . .*" Western settlers had every reason to hate those easterners who portrayed them as uncivilized.

Differences between life for settlers on the western frontier and those in the east soon divided people of the colony, with some supporting the plantation owners and government officials of the east and others siding with the farmers of the west.

The western protesters became known as the Regulators as it was their intent to fight what they called a "War of Regulation" to control the tax collectors and create reform. At first, they sent letters to Governor Tryon complaining about their treatment. They also held public protests, but little was done to address their concerns. In 1770, they issued a proclamation:

> [We will] assemble . . . for conference for regulating public grievances and abuses of power. We will pay no more taxes until we are satisfied that they are agreeable to law, and applied to the purposes therein mentioned, unless we cannot help it, or are forced. We will pay no officer any more fees than the law allows. . . .

In August 1770, Edmund Fanning, a tax collector, seized the horse and saddle of one of the Regulators, intending to sell it to pay taxes that the colonist owed. Soon afterward, a group of Regulators rode into the town of Hillsboro, fired several shots into Fanning's home, and retook the horse. Unable to locate those responsible, Fanning had two Regulator leaders, William Butler and Hermon Husband, arrested.

The next day, more than 700 men marched to the town jail and demanded the release of Butler and Husband. Fanning and other officials, afraid of the mob, released the prisoners and fled.

Royal Governor Tyron, backed by colonial militiamen, orders a group of Regulators to put down their weapons and disassemble.

THE REGULATOR WAR

News of the situation reached Governor Tryon. On his request, the assembly gave him permission to use the colonial militia to restore order to the region. Colonists who agreed with the Regulators traveled to Orange County and the surrounding areas to support them.

militia—a group of citizen volunteers organized for military service

By April 1771, Tryon had raised a militia of nearly 1,000 men. The Regulators and those who had come to aid them numbered more than 2,000. Most of the Regulators lacked military training, while Tryon's force included some trained soldiers and officers.

On May 16, Tryon's militia met the Regulator force at a place called Alamance in Orange County. After less than two hours of battle, the Regulators and their supporters surrendered. After their defeat, as many as 1,500 Regulators left North Carolina, settling in the land that would become the states of Kentucky and Tennessee.

After the Regulator War, there was a rising feeling of distrust between colonists and the British government. In August 1774, colonial leaders from North Carolina met in New Bern, in what was later called the First Provincial Congress. They drafted a document listing British acts and policies to which they objected. They also selected colonial delegates to send to Philadelphia to the First Continental Congress, a meeting of representatives from each colony to discuss the growing conflict between the colonists and the British government.

delegates—people elected or selected to represent others

The North Carolina assembly became a center for debate and complaint about British policy, so on April 8, 1775, the newly elected Governor Martin ordered it disbanded. The colonists were furious. But before they could organize any protest against the governor, momentous news arrived. On the morning of April 19, on a field in Lexington, Massachusetts, a band of colonists had exchanged fire with a group of British soldiers. The Colonies were at war with Great Britain.

North Carolina in the Revolution

THE BRITISH BELIEVE NORTH CAROLINA *will remain loyal, but Patriots soon overpower British troops and their Loyalist allies. The Battle at Guilford Courthouse helps decide the war's eventual outcome.*

As news of the fighting in Massachusetts spread through the Colonies, many people loyal to the King began to fear for their safety. Governor Martin and his family fled New Bern on the evening of May 24, 1775. They rode to Fort Johnson, a British fort near the mouth of the Cape Fear River. Martin put his family on a

OPPOSITE: General Nathanael Greene readies his troops for crossing the low waters of the Dan River in order to evade the British in February 1781, during the Revolutionary War.

ship to New York. He then wrote to General Thomas Gage, leader of the British forces in the Colonies.

He reported that the Patriot colonists were *"setting up a system of rule and regulation"* that was a threat to the King's rule. He also noted that he had the men and support needed *"to maintain the sovereignty of this country to my royal master in any event,"* but asked Gage to supply him with guns and ammunition. Patriots intercepted the letter and soon located the governor. They attacked Fort Johnson, eventually burning it to the ground, but Martin escaped to the *Cruizer*, a British warship.

MOORES CREEK BRIDGE

On the ship, Martin began planning how the British could regain control of North Carolina. The British would need to retake the port of Brunswick. Controlling the port would allow him to receive supplies and strike out at Patriot militias in surrounding towns.

Martin believed he could convince many of the residents of Cape Fear to support the British. He sent messengers promising whoever fought for Britain would receive 200 acres (81 ha) of land and freedom from taxes for 20 years. But many of the Scots and Irish living in Cape Fear had supported the Regulators and were distrustful of the British. By February 15, 1776, Martin had raised a force of more than 1,500 Loyalists, far less than the 10,000 he had hoped to recruit.

Loyalists—colonists who remained loyal to Britain; also known as Tories

At the same time, the Patriots were busy raising an army of their own, concentrating their force near Wilmington. Word arrived that the British Army was planning to make its way to the coast through Wilmington. The Patriots moved to block the British at a bridge that crossed Moores Creek 20 miles (32 km) outside of Wilmington.

A Patriot militia of 150 men under the command of Colonel Alexander Lillington arrived at the bridge first and prepared an ambush. His men loosened and removed planks from the bridge.

ambush—a surprise
attack

They were soon joined by a force of 850 men commanded by Colonel Richard Caswell.

Before daybreak on the morning of February 27, the Loyalists, 1,500 strong, approached the bridge. Captain John Campbell selected 75 men to lead the attack on the Patriots. His plan was to rush across the bridge, begin the attack, and then have the rest of the Loyalist troops join the fight. The 75 Loyalists had nearly made it across the half-destroyed bridge when the entire Patriot force opened fire. The first volley killed 30 and wounded 40 of the 75 Loyalists. Shocked, the Loyalists retreated. Within several weeks, Patriot forces captured the remainder of the Loyalist troops. Only one Patriot died in all this fighting.

volley—a round of
shots

With North Carolina securely in American hands, many of the militiamen went off to fight in other battles throughout the Colonies.

The Provincial Congress

On April 12, 1776, the 86 delegates to the Provincial Congress drafted and approved a document that came to be known as the Halifax Resolves. The document provided *"that the delegates for this Colony in the Continental Congress be empowered to concur with the delegates of the other Colonies in declaring Independency."*

On August 2, Joseph Hewes, William Hooper, and John Penn, North Carolina's delegates to the Continental Congress, signed the Declaration of Independence. On December 18, the Provincial Congress adopted North Carolina's first state constitution. Shortly afterward, it elected Richard Caswell as the first governor of the new state.

THE CHEROKEE THREAT

With the outbreak of open warfare between the colonists and Great Britain, the Cherokee again found themselves in the middle of a war. They were unsure which side to support. In June 1776, the British offered to protect Cherokee territory from future expansion by the colonists if the Cherokee agreed to fight for the British in the war. The Cherokee agreed and began raiding colonial outposts and attacking small towns.

Angered by the Cherokee decision to align with the British, the Americans sent General Griffith Rutherford and 2,400 men to invade Cherokee lands. Within months Rutherford's force destroyed 32 Cherokee towns and villages and forced them to surrender. They agreed to give up land in what is present-day Tennessee and to no longer support the British.

THE BRITISH SOUTHERN STRATEGY

In 1780, most of the southern colonies were full of Loyalists who, the British believed, would support them if the Patriots were defeated. On May 12, 1780, a British force of 7,800 under General Henry Clinton captured Charleston, South Carolina. A few Loyalists joined the British troops, but not as many as the British expected.

After his victory, Clinton was called to New York. He left his army under the command of Lord Charles Cornwallis, who began planning a British invasion of North Carolina.

On May 18, Cornwallis ordered his army to begin marching north toward the North Carolina border. He remained in Charleston to oversee the strategy. News of the British approach encouraged Loyalists across North Carolina to rally. Some Loyalists formed small armies and attempted to join up with the advancing British troops, but, in most cases, Patriot forces stopped the Loyalists before they reached the British.

News of the British approach reached General Horatio Gates, commander of American forces in the south. He moved his army of 1,500 trained soldiers and 1,500 militiamen to block the British march into North Carolina. On August 14, Cornwallis joined his army of 1,500 British soldiers and 500 Loyalist militiamen at Camden. The

British and Patriots lined up their forces, and on the morning of August 16, Gates ordered his men to open fire.

The victorious British lost 324 men at the battle of Camden, but the rebels lost more than a thousand, with another thousand taken prisoner. At least 400 of the dead were militiamen from North Carolina. Gates escaped, but was replaced as commander of American forces in the south by General Nathanael Greene.

In this painting by artist Howard Pyle, General Nathanael Greene meets General Horatio Gates at Gates' headquarters in Charlotte, North Carolina, in 1780.

Cornwallis pushed north through North Carolina in preparation for an attack on Virginia. He ordered a force of Loyalist militiamen under the command of Major Patrick Ferguson to scout ahead of his main group, to root out Patriots who had fled the battles of Charleston and Camden and to protect his main force from ambush.

Ferguson was a well-trained soldier and an excellent hunter, but his troops were not well trained. As they advanced through North Carolina, they were confronted with many small ambushes by Patriot forces. Ferguson set up camp near Gilbert Town in late August. He sent letters to Patriot militia leaders Colonel Isaac Shelby and Colonel John Sevier, who were both in Sullivan County, North Carolina (now part of present-day Tennessee). Ferguson's letters said that if the Patriots did not surrender to the British forces, he *"would march his army over the mountains, hang their leaders, and lay their country waste with fire and sword."*

THE BATTLE OF KINGS MOUNTAIN

Ferguson's letter angered Sevier and Shelby. They decided to quickly raise a militia and attack Ferguson before he could be reinforced. They sent out word to surrounding counties. By September 25, 1780, they had gathered a force of almost 1,400. The next day, they began the march toward Ferguson's Loyalists.

When news of the advancing Patriot militia reached Ferguson, he ordered his force of nearly 1,000 to retreat to Kings Mountain, about 20 miles (32 km) south of Gilbert Town. There, Ferguson prepared to defend the mountaintop.

The Patriot militia reached Kings Mountain at midday and prepared to attack. Although untrained, most of the Patriots were excellent marksmen. Sevier and Shelby decided that rather than attack in rows, as most armies did, they would form smaller groups that would attack the Loyalists from all sides, using the cover of rocks and trees.

As the battle began, Loyalists took fire from three sides. After nearly an hour of fighting, the Patriots reached the top of the mountain. There they sighted Ferguson, a tall man wearing a bright shirt and using a whistle to command his troops. He was an easy target for the Patriot marksmen. Many witnesses said that when Ferguson fell from his horse, he was dead before he hit the ground, his body spotted with bullet holes.

With their leader dead, the Loyalists soon surrendered. In little more than an hour, a group of largely untrained soldiers had killed 225 Loyalist troops and wounded 163. More than 700 were taken prisoner. Only 28 Patriots were killed.

News of the defeat reached Cornwallis. Without Ferguson to protect his advance, Cornwallis fell back to South Carolina, giving General Greene time to organize and supply the Patriot forces in the south.

This painting shows the First Maryland Regiment fighting with General Greene's force against the British at Guilford Courthouse.

THE RACE TO THE DAN AND THE BATTLE AT GUILFORD COURTHOUSE

Cornwallis was angered by the defeat at Kings Mountain. Had his troops won, he would have been able to press into North Carolina and battle Greene's weaker army. In December 1780, Cornwallis resupplied, and left South Carolina with more than 2,000 British troops. His mission was to track down Greene and destroy his force.

General Greene was considered by many to be the greatest tactical leader in the American Revolution. In the winter of 1780, his force numbered less than 2,000, most of whom were poorly trained volunteers. He knew that a direct attack on Cornwallis could not be successful. Rather than fight, Greene took his troops across North Carolina. He kept his army close enough to Cornwallis's army that they could easily follow him, but Greene avoided battles. Each mile north that Cornwallis marched in North Carolina moved him farther from his supplies in South Carolina.

tactical—relating to battle plans

By mid-February, Greene had led Cornwallis to the Dan River on the Virginia border. Planning to cross the river and meet reinforcements in Virginia, Greene sent men ahead to build boats. When his main force arrived, it was quickly ferried across the river. Cornwallis knew it would take weeks for his British troops to build enough boats to cross the river, so he retreated to Hillsboro, North Carolina.

By early March, Greene had received reinforcements. His force now numbered more than 4,000. He recrossed the Dan River and headed south. His forces intercepted Cornwallis at Guilford Courthouse in present-day Greensboro, North Carolina, on March 15, 1781.

After hours of fighting, Greene ordered his men to retreat. The British could not organize quickly enough to pursue them. That evening, a driving rain further prevented the British from chasing Greene, and his army escaped.

Though the battle was a British victory, it was a costly one. More than 450 of Cornwallis's men were killed, compared to only about 250 of the Patriots. When news of the British victory reached London, Charles James Fox, a leader in Parliament, commented, *"Another such victory would ruin the British Army."*

Pyle's "HACKING MATCH"

ACROSS NORTH CAROLINA AND THE OTHER COLONIES, small bands of Loyalists prepared to fight the Patriot forces. Dr. John Pyle, a known Loyalist, lived in northern North Carolina. As news spread of Cornwallis's approach, he recruited a Loyalist militia of nearly 400 men and made plans to join Cornwallis's main force. On the afternoon of February 24, 1781, however, General Andrew Pickens and Lieutenant Colonel Henry Lee, commanding Patriot troops in the region, learned of Pyle's location.

Pickens knew that his much larger force could easily overpower the Loyalists, so he sent Lee ahead to the Loyalist camp to demand Pyle's surrender. Pyle's untrained men welcomed Lee, mistaking his force for allies due to a likeness in their uniforms. Lee identified himself and demanded Pyle's surrender. Instead of surrendering, however, some of Pyle's men attacked Lee's force.

The men fought in close combat, using bayonets, knives, and swords. By the time Lee regained control, nearly 100 Loyalists were dead. Lee's force suffered a single casualty— a horse. Pyle was taken prisoner. None of his men ever met up with Cornwallis's army.

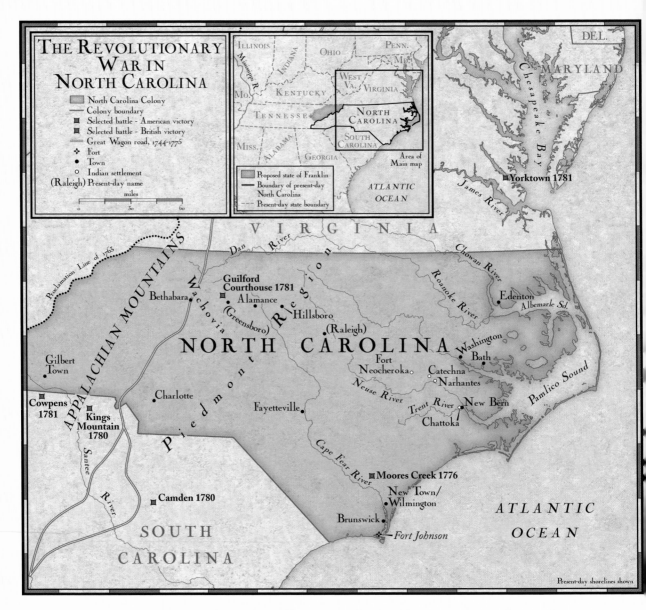

THE REVOLUTIONARY WAR IN NORTH CAROLINA

North Carolina Colony
Colony boundary
Selected battle - American victory
Selected battle - British victory
Great Wagon road, 1744-1775
Fort
Town
Indian settlement
(Raleigh) Present-day name

miles
0   30   60

Proposed state of Franklin
Boundary of present-day North Carolina
Present-day state boundary

Area of Main map

ATLANTIC OCEAN

ILLINOIS INDIANA OHIO PENN. MD.
MO. KENTUCKY WEST VA. VIRGINIA
TENNESSEE NORTH CAROLINA
MISS. ALABAMA GEORGIA SOUTH CAROLINA
Mississippi R.

DEL.
MARYLAND
Chesapeake Bay

Yorktown 1781

James River

Chowan River

VIRGINIA

Dan River

Roanoke River

Proclamation Line of 1763

APPALACHIAN MOUNTAINS

Wachovia

Bethabara
Guilford Courthouse 1781
Alamance
(Greensboro)
Hillsboro

(Raleigh)

Edenton
Albemarle Sd.

Washington
Bath

NORTH CAROLINA

Piedmont Region

Gilbert Town

Fort Neocheroka
Catechna
Narhantes

Neuse River

Charlotte

Fayetteville

Trent River
Chattoka

New Bern

Pamlico Sound

Cowpens 1781

Kings Mountain 1780

Santee River

Piedmont

Cape Fear River

Moores Creek 1776

New Town/
Wilmington

ATLANTIC OCEAN

Camden 1780

Brunswick

Fort Johnson

SOUTH CAROLINA

Present-day shorelines shown

The Revolutionary War didn't heat up in North Carolina until summer 1780. That's when General Nathanael Greene took command of American forces in the South after the British under Cornwallis scored major victories at Charleston and Camden. The Patriots got revenge at Kings Mountain and Cowpens, and Greene led Cornwallis on a lengthy chase through the backcountry of North Carolina that ended at Guilford Courthouse. Greene's troops were defeated but helped bring about the end of the war by causing an exhausted Cornwallis to leave North Carolina and head for Yorktown.

CORNWALLIS MOVES NORTH AS GREENE MOVES SOUTH

Cornwallis's army was in desperate need of reinforcements, so he headed east to Wilmington, where he hoped to find supplies and recruits.

Meanwhile, Greene moved his army south and began retaking towns in North and South Carolina that had fallen to the British.

Realizing he had lost control of the Carolinas, Cornwallis decided to push north into Virginia and meet up with other British forces there. Reaching Yorktown, his troops quickly began fortifying the town.

The Americans acted quickly. With aid from the French—who had agreed to help the Americans fight the British—they blocked the port at Yorktown, cutting off Cornwallis's supplies and eliminating any chance for escape by sea. An American and French force that numbered nearly 19,000, under the command of General George Washington, approached Yorktown. Smaller Patriot forces from across the Colonies moved into strategic positions around Yorktown. By the end of September, Cornwallis found himself surrounded.

On October 9, the American and French forces began bombarding the British. Cut off from supplies, running short on food, and with no reinforcements in sight, Cornwallis surrendered his army on October 19.

CHAPTER EIGHT

Toward Statehood

THE REVOLUTIONARY WAR ENDS, *but North Carolina has difficulty uniting its citizens. The new state ratifies the U.S. Constitution after insisting a Bill of Rights be added.*

fter Cornwallis surrendered, it was only a matter of time before Britain accepted defeat. The surrender at Yorktown cost the British more than a third of their army in America. They were now outnumbered and no match for the combined American and French forces.

On September 3, 1783, Great Britain and the United States signed the Treaty of Paris, officially ending the

OPPOSITE: British General Charles O'Hara (center, foreground) surrenders Cornwallis's sword to the Continental Army's General Benjamin Lincoln (in blue coat) at Yorktown, Virginia, on October 19, 1781.

American Revolution. On January 14, 1784, Congress ratified the treaty. Britain prepared to transport its soldiers and many Loyalists out of the United States.

Congress—the legislative body of the U.S. Government

THE SHORT-LIVED STATE OF FRANKLIN

In early 1784, Congress asked the states to help pay debts the new nation had incurred during the war for independence. In April 1784, North Carolina's assembly considered its options. The Revolution had proved costly for many people. Soldiers often went unpaid, and farmers and merchants had not made money while away fighting a war. Instead of imposing taxes that few could pay, the assembly offered to give Congress land, which it could either sell to another state or use in whatever way seemed most profitable. The assembly offered 29 million acres (11.7 million ha) of land between the Appalachian Mountains and the Mississippi River, land in present-day Tennessee. The suggestion so angered the region's residents that North Carolina soon decided to take back its offer.

Still, people living in the area were not happy. On August 23, 1784, delegates from across the region met in the town of Jonesborough. They decided that their only option was to declare themselves independent of North Carolina. They set up a temporary government and selected

John Sevier as governor. They called the land the State of Franklin, to honor Benjamin Franklin, a famous Patriot. On May 16, 1785, they sent delegates to Congress to ask to be recognized as an independent state, but Congress voted to reject their request.

This put the State of Franklin in a difficult situation. It could not rely on getting military support or supplies from either the United States or from North Carolina. To protect the small state, its leaders began making treaties with the surrounding Indian groups. Franklin also began looking to France and Spain for support.

The government in North Carolina did not like the idea of the State of Franklin negotiating with foreign countries. It offered to accept Franklin back into North Carolina and to cancel any back taxes its citizens owed in North Carolina. Franklin's government rejected the offer.

In 1787, North Carolina sent troops to the region to force Franklin to rejoin the state. Governor Sevier raised a small army but put up little resistance. By early 1788, Franklin had been persuaded to rejoin North

John Sevier, Governor of the State of Franklin

Carolina. In 1796, North Carolina would again give up the region, this time to form what would become the state of Tennessee. Sevier became that state's first governor.

SLAVE LAWS

THE FIRST SLAVERY LAWS IN NORTH CAROLINA DATE BACK to 1715, when the assembly decided that slaves, free blacks, and Indians would not have the right to vote. King George II overruled this law in 1737, allowing free blacks to vote in the colony. In 1741, the assembly made a law requiring all newly freed slaves to leave North Carolina within six months of being freed. Soon after, plantation owners in the Cape Fear area began importing slaves from Africa to work the fields. When the American Revolution began, the British announced that all slaves were free and recruited them to fight for Britain. Many blacks joined the British forces and left the state with the defeated British Army at the end of the Revolution. Others were forced to stay on by their masters, or had a greater fear of leaving to fight a war in which they might be killed.

In December 1785, the assembly passed a law requiring that all slaves in the towns of Edenton, Fayetteville, Washington, and Wilmington wear lead badges that identified them as property. Every free black who remained in the state was required to wear a cloth armband with the word "free" written across it.

By 1790, nearly a quarter of the state's population consisted of black slaves. That number continued to grow.

A New Constitution

On September 17, 1787, three North Carolina delegates to the Constitutional Convention—William Blount, Richard Dobbs Spaight, and Hugh Williamson—signed the U.S. Constitution. After its signing, the document was sent to each state, where a state convention was held and a vote was taken to ratify or reject the Constitution.

Delegates at the North Carolina state convention objected to the Constitution because it did not include a list of guaranteed rights and protections for citizens. The delegates feared that without this, the federal government would become too strong. On August 2, 1788, North Carolina's delegates decided they would not ratify the document until it included specific laws designed to limit the powers of the government while guarding the freedoms of the people. Under pressure from North Carolina, and other state conventions, Congress agreed to add ten laws, collectively known as the Bill of Rights, to the Constitution. James Madison, a delegate from Virginia, drafted the document, outlining such basic freedoms as freedom of speech, freedom of the press, and freedom of religious worship. On September 25, 1789, Congress ratified the Bill of Rights, making it part of the Constitution. North Carolina's delegates were now satisfied that the rights of citizens would be protected. On November 21, North Carolina became the 12th state to ratify the U.S. Constitution.

The UNIVERSITY of NORTH CAROLINA

IN 1776, THE ASSEMBLY CALLED FOR THE CONSTRUCTION OF a university in North Carolina where *"all useful learning shall be duly encouraged and promoted."* But the Revolutionary War put the plans on hold. It was not until 1789 that the assembly granted a charter for the University of North Carolina at Chapel Hill. The first building, now called "Old East," was completed in 1795. In February of that year, it became the first public university in the United States to admit students.

A NEW CAPITAL

In 1790, a census listed North Carolina's population at 393,751. Of this total, 288,204 people were white, 100,572 were slaves, and 4,975 were other free people, including free blacks.

Not only was the population growing, but people had begun settling far inland. New Bern was no longer a central location, and Tryon Palace had been neglected. It had been damaged during the Revolution and had caught fire several times. The assembly decided to build a new capital city. After some debate, the assembly ordered that Wake County should be the site of the state's new capital.

In early 1792, Joel Lane, a landowner in North Carolina, agreed to sell 1,000 acres (405 ha) of his land in Wake County to the state to be used for North Carolina's new capital city. The assembly decided to name the new capital Raleigh in honor of Sir Walter Ralegh, who had attempted to establish the first settlement in the colony more than 200 years earlier.

That they chose the site of Raleigh was fitting. After all, it was named for a man who had envisioned the hopeful possibilities for English settlement in the New World. North Carolina was and would continue to be a place where men and women from Europe and Great Britain would try to make something of their lives.

This U.S. flag is known as the Guilford Courthouse flag because it was raised over the Guilford Courthouse by General Greene's troops on March 15, 1781. North Carolina did not have an official state flag until 1861.

TIME LINE

1500   More than 50,000 Indians live in what would become North Carolina.

1524   Giovanni da Verrazano lands at present-day Cape Fear, North Carolina.

1540   Hernando de Soto explores North Carolina.

1570   Fewer than 15,000 Indians remain in North Carolina after disease destroys their tribes.

1584   Sir Walter Ralegh receives a patent to found a colony in North America.

1585   A colony is established on Roanoke Island but abandoned within a year.

1587   Ralegh's second colonial expedition, under the command of Governor John White, lands at Roanoke.

1590   White returns to Roanoke but finds no trace of the colonists he left the previous year.

1607   English investors establish the Jamestown colony in Virginia.

1629   King Charles I gives a patent to Sir Robert Heath to colonize Carolina, but Heath does little to settle the area.

1660   King Charles II rewards eight of his supporters by giving them the title Lord Proprietor and a patent to colonize Carolina.

1670   Charleston in present-day South Carolina becomes the first city in Carolina and capital of the colony.

1673   The English government passes the Plantation Duty Act, requiring all colonies to trade directly with England.

1679   John Culpeper and George Durant lead a group of supporters who capture English officials in what becomes known as Culpeper's Rebellion.

1700-1730   Immigration into North Carolina accelerates as settlers from the New England colonies and western Europe push south.

1704   Bath, the first town in what is now North Carolina, is founded.

1705   Parliament passes the Naval Stores Act.

1711   The Tuscarora War begins.

1713   The Tuscarora are defeated at Fort Neoheroka, ending the Tuscarora War.

1729   North Carolina becomes a royal colony.

1745   The colonial assembly selects New Bern as the capital of North Carolina.

1754   The French and Indian War begins.

1763   The Treaty of Paris ends the French and Indian War.

1765   Parliament passes the Stamp Act.

1766   Construction begins on the governor's residence in New Bern.

1771   Governor William Tryon commands the North Carolina militia against the Regulators.

1774   Colonial leaders at North Carolina's First Provincial Congress agree to send delegates to the First Continental Congress.

1775   Fighting breaks out between Patriots and British troops in Lexington and Concord, Massachusetts. In North Carolina, Patriots try to capture Governor Josiah Martin, but he escapes.

1776   Patriots defeat Loyalists and British troops at the Battle of Moores Creek Bridge.

1780   British troops capture Charleston, South Carolina, and continue north into North Carolina.

1781   On March 15, American forces attack British troops at Guilford Courthouse (present-day Greensboro). On October 9, the battle of Yorktown begins. On October 19th, the British surrender at Yorktown.

1783   Britain and the United States sign the Treaty of Paris, officially ending the American Revolution.

1787   Three delegates from North Carolina sign the U.S. Constitution.

1788   The North Carolina state assembly votes against ratifying the Constitution because it does not include a list of citizen rights.

1789   After the Bill of Rights is added to the Constitution, the North Carolina Assembly becomes the 12th state to ratify the Constitution.

RESOURCES

BOOKS

Rankin, Hugh F. *The Pirates of Colonial North Carolina*. Raleigh: North Carolina Department of Cultural Resources, 1989.

Powell, William S. *North Carolina: A History* Chapel Hill: University of North Carolina Press, 1998.

Fradin, Dennis B. *North Carolina Colony (The Thirteen Colonies)*. New York: Children's Press, 1991.

Margulies, Phillip. *A Primary Source History of the Colony of North Carolina*. New York: Rosen Central, 2005.

Miller, Brandon Marie. *Good Women of a Well-Blessed Land: Women's Lives in Colonial America*. Minneapolis: Lerner Publications, 2003.

WEB SITES

The State Library of North Carolina
http://statelibrary.dcr.state.nc.us/NC/HISTORY/HISTORY.HTM

North Carolina History
http://www.secretary.state.nc.us/kidspg/history.htm

North Carolina Museum of History
http://ncmuseumofhistory.org/

North Carolina History Project
http://www.northcarolinahistory.org/

North Carolina Native Americans
http://www.archaeolink.com/first_nations_north_carolina_ind.htm

Indian Tribal Records
http://www.accessgenealogy.com/native/northcarolina/index.htm

North Carolina Maritime Museum
http://www.ah.dcr.state.nc.us/sections/maritime/Blackbeard/default.htm

Quote Sources

CHAPTER ONE

p. 15 "there appeared...on the seashore." Wroth, Lawrence C., editor. *The Voyages of Giovanni da Verrazzano, 1524–1528.* Connecticut: Yale University Press, 1970, pp. 133–143; p. 16 "They go...on the high seas." Wroth, pp. 133–143; p. 22 "The next day...much he had." Clayton, Lawrence A., Vernon James Knight, Jr., and Edward Moore. *The DeSoto Chronicles: The Expedition of Hernando De Soto to North America in 1539–1543,* Tuscaloosa, AL: University of Alabama Press, 1993; p. 6; " They found...over two days." Clayton, Knight, and Moore.

CHAPTER TWO

p. 25 "to discover, search...Christian People." http://fordham.edu/halsall/mod; p. 27 "very sandy and...not to be found." National Park Service Historical Handbook #15, Fort Raleigh. Washington, D.C.: U.S. Government Printing Office, 1954; p. 29 "It may be...true religion." Stevens, Henry. *Thomas Harriot.* Whitefish, Montana: Kessinger Publishing, 2004, p. 68; p. 31 "courteous...have clothes." National Park Service Historical Handbook #15; p. 32 "unwilling to...long held." National Park Service Historical Handbook #15; p. 35 "the houses stand...those melons." National Park Service Historical Handbook #15.

CHAPTER THREE

p. 39 "fruit, wooden spears...fragrance." Borio, Gene. *The Tobacco Timeline.* Accessed at http://www.tobacco.org/History/Tobacco_History.html; p. 40 "poor and...taste." Poff, Jan-Michael. *Upheaval in Albermarle: The Story of Culpeper's Rebellion.* Accessed at http://www.ah.dcr.state.nc.us/section/hp/Colonial/Bookshelf/Monographs/upheaval/upheaval1.htm, paragraph 3; "sweet-scented" Poff, paragraph 3; p. 41 "far more temperate...more quantity." Bland, Edward. *The Virginia Indian Trade to 1673.* Accessed at http://www.dinsdoc.com/morrison-1.htm, p. 230; p. 42 "All that Territory...South Seas aforesaid;" *History Highlights of North Carolina.* Accessed at http://state library.dcr.state.nc.US/NC/HISTORY/HISTORY.HTM, paragraph 15; p. 51 "of the Principall Contrivers...in Carolina." Poff, paragraph 3.

CHAPTER FOUR

p. 54 "very regular...brick and wood." Lawson, John. *A New Voyage to Carolina; Containing the Exact Descroption and Natural History of that Country: Together with the Present Sate Thereof. And a Journal of a Thousand Miles, Travel'd Thro' Several Nations of Indians. Giving a Particular Account of their customs, Manners, &c.* London: W. Taylor and J. Baker, 1714. Accessed at http://www.amphilsoc.org/library/exhibits/nature/lawson.htm; p. 55 "They are...doors hungry." Gally, Alan, editor. *Voices of the Old South.* Athens, Georgia: University of Georgia Press, 1994, p. 38; "[Local Indians were]...into the water." Gally, p. 40; p. 57 "cheated these Indians...plantations." Lee, E. Lawrence. *Indian Wars in North Carolina, 1663–1763.* Raleigh, North Carolina: Carolina Charter Tercenteny Commission, 1963, paragraph 3; "stuck him...on fire." Lee, paragraph 5; p. 59 "until most...the sword." Lee, paragraph 17.

CHAPTER FIVE

pp. 66–67 "I see this...my own employment." Johnson, Lloyd. *The Welsh in Carolina in the Eighteenth Century.* Accessed at http://spruce.flint.umich.edu/~ellisjs/Lloyd2.pdf, paragraph 1; p. 67 "consisting of not...a village." Johnson, Accessed at http://spruce.flint.umich.edu/~ellisjs/Lloyd2.pdf, paragraph 2; "arrived very poor...with his family." Gally, Alan, editor. *Voices of the Old South.* Athens, Georgia: University of Georgia Press, 1994, p. 125; p. 69 "produce the same...trouble to yourself." Gally, pp. 69–70; p. 71 "The importance of...all we can do." Gally, p. 46; p. 72 "By whose authority...peaceable departure." Ockershausen, Jane. *Forts at the Forks: Frontier History Comes to Life at the Fort Pitt Museum.* Accessed at http://www.phmc.state.pa.us/ppet/pitt/page1.asp?secid=31, paragraph 2; "As to the...to obey." Ockershausen, paragraph 2.

CHAPTER SIX

p. 76 "all Civil...at a stand." http://www.ncmuseumofhistory.org/nchh/eighteenth.html, paragraph 110; p. 77 "the most beautiful...colonies." Carraway, Gertrude Sprague. *Tryon's Palace: North Carolina's First State Capital.* Raleigh, North Carolina: State Department of Archives and History, 1945, Accessed at http://statelibrary.dcr.state.nc.us/nc/ncsites/tryon.htm, paragraph 2; "a lasting...country." Carraway, paragraph 20; p. 78 "They are...or handkerchiefs" Gally, Alan, Editor. *Voices of the Old South.* Athens, Georgia: University of Georgia Press, 1995, p. 132; p. 79 "[We will] assemble...the law allows." Henderson, Archibald. "Origin of the Regulation in North Carolina." *American Historical Review.* 21: 1916, pp. 320–32.

CHAPTER SEVEN

p. 84 "setting up...regulation." http://www.famousamericans.net/josiahmartin/; "to maintain...any event." http://www.famousamericans.net/josiahmartin/; p. 86 "that the delegates...declaring Independency." http://statelibrary.acr.state.nc.us/nc/history/history.htm#Halifax, paragraph 27; p.89 "would march his...fire and sword." http://www.tngenweb.org/revwar/kingsmountain.html, paragraph 2; p. 93 "Another such...British Army." http://www.williamsresearch.net/TheRaceToTheDan.html.

CHAPTER EIGHT

p. 102 "all useful learning...and promoted." http://www.unc.edu/about/history.html, paragraph 1.

INDEX

ABOUT THE AUTHOR AND CONSULTANT

MATTHEW C. CANNAVALE has written and edited numerous books for middle-grade readers, including several biographies and historical accounts. He received undergraduate degrees in English and secondary education and has a graduate degree from the Harvard Graduate School of Education. He is also the author of *Voices from Colonial America: Florida: 1513–1821.*

PATRICK GRIFFIN is a professor at the University of Virginia. He earned his Ph.D. at Northwestern University. He has published books on the Colonies and the people who settled them, including *American Leviathan: Empire, Nation, and Revolutionary Frontier* and *The People with No Name: Ireland's Ulster Scots, America's Scots Irish, and the Creation of a British Atlantic World, 1689–1764.* He lives in Charlottesville, Virginia, with his wife and four children.

ILLUSTRATION CREDITS